COMPARATIVE TABLES OF ISLAMIC AND CHRISTIAN DATES

Enabling one to find exact equivalent of any day in any month from the beginning of the Muhammadan era

COMPILED BY

L.T.-COLONEL SIR WOLSELEY HAIG

K.C I.E., C.S I., C.M.G , C.B.E., M.A. (DUBLIN)

KITAB BHAVAN

NEW DELHI.110002

Kitab Bhavan
Publishers, Distributors, Exporters & Importers
1784, Kalan Mahal, Darya Ganj
New Delhi - 1100 02 [India]

Phone	:	(91-11) 23277392/93, 23274686, 30906494
Mobile	:	(91-11) 9910114484
website	:	www.kitabbhavan.com
Email	:	nasri@vsnl.com, nusrat@bol.net.in
Fax	:	(91-11) 23263383

Edition 2006

ISBN : 81-7151-085-X
Book Code No. C00009

Published in India by :
Nusrat Ali Nasri for Kitab Bhavan
1784, Kalan Mahal, Darya Ganj
New Delhi - 1100 02 [India]

Printed in India at :
Lahooti Fine Art Press
1711, Sui Walan, Darya Ganj
New Delhi - 110002 [India]

INTRODUCTION

THE following tables are intended for students of Oriental history who are able to use original authorities, to enable them readily to convert dates in the lunar years of the Muhammadan era of the *Hijra* into their corresponding dates in the Christian era.

The first table contains three columns. The first column contains every year of the era of the *Hijra* from its beginning on July 16, A.D. 622, down to the end of the twentieth century. The second column gives the years of the Christian era, leap years being marked with an asterisk, and the date in each year on which the corresponding year of the era of the *Hijra* began. The third gives the number of the days of each Christian year which had elapsed before the year of the *Hijra* began. The second table gives the months of the Christian year and the consecutive numbers of days of both common and leap years. The third gives the months of the year in the era of the *Hijra* and the consecutive numbers of days of the year.

The method of using the tables can best be explained by examples. Let it be supposed that we wish to find the date in the Christian era corresponding to *Rajab* 10, A.H. 722. The student first looks up the year 722 in the first column of Table I and finds that it began on January 20, A.D. 1322, nineteen days of the Christian year having elapsed before it began. He sets down the figures 19, and, turning to Table III, finds that Rajab 10 is the 187th day of the *Hijra* year. He then adds 187 to 19, obtaining the sum 206. Turning to Table II he finds that the 206th day of the Christian year, not being a leap year, is July 25. Therefore the Christian date corresponding to Rajab 10, A.H. 722, is July 25, 1322.

But it often happens that a year of the *Hijra* goes far beyond the Christian year in which it began. Let us suppose, for instance, that we wish to find the date in the Christian era corresponding to Ramadan 5, A.H. 966. In Table I we find that the year 966 of the era of the *Hijra* began on October 14, 1558, when 286 days of the year had elapsed. Setting down the figures 286 we find, on reference to Table III, that Ramadan 5 is the 241st day of the lunar year. Adding 241 to 286 we get the sum 527, reckoned from January 1, 1558. From this we subtract 365, the number of days in the Christian year 1558, and find that the remainder is 162. Ramadan 5, 966, is therefore the 162nd day of the Christian year following 1558, that is, as we discover from Table II, June 11, 1559.

When a year of the era of the *Hijra* begins in a leap year of the Christian era and extends beyond that year, it must be remembered that the number to be deducted from the sum of the days of the Christian year and those of the *Hijra* year, is 366, not 365: thus, if we wish to find the Christian date corresponding to Rajab 3, 1096, we find first that the year 1096 of the *Hijra* began on December 8, 1684, a leap year, of which 342 days had elapsed before the *Hijra* year began. Rajab 3, being the 180th day of the lunar year we add 180 to 342, obtaining the sum 522. The Christian year 1684 contained 366 days and we subtract 366 from 522, leaving the remainder 156. Thus, Rajab 3, 1096, corresponds to the 156th day of the Christian year 1685, that is, to June 5, 1685, as we discover from Table II.

It must be remembered that the Muhammadan day, like the Biblical day, and the ecclesiastical day of the Christian Church, begins at sunset, so that what we call Thursday evening a Muslim will call Friday evening, and if a Muslim historian says that a certain event happened on the night of Safar 3, 1069 (October 31, 1658) it may have happened between sunset and midnight on October 30, or between midnight and dawn on October 31.

One more word is necessary regarding the Old and New Styles of the Christian calendar. By 1582 it had been discovered that in the Julian calendar the length of the year had been sligtly miscalculated, with the result that the days of the month were by then ten days in advance of the true dates. Pope Gregory XIII therefore reformed the Christian calendar and corrected the dates by omitting ten days from 1582, so that the *Hijra* year 991, which, had the Christian year not been altered, would have begun on January 15, began on January 25, 1583, according to the New, or Gregorian Style. Pope Gregory's reform of the calendar was gradually adopted by all countries in Europe, except England, Russia and Sweden. Russia, in her ecclesiastical calendar, still follows the Julian, or Old Style, but Britain reformed her calendar in 1752, by suppressing eleven days between September 2 and 14, so that the third day of that month in that year became the fourteenth. Pope Gregory's reform consisted besides the excision of ten days in 1582, in a change in the reckoning of leap years. In the Julian calendar every fourth year was a leap year, but in the Gregorian calendar century years are not leap years unless their first two figures are divisible by four. Thus 1600 was a leap year and 2000 will be a leap year, but 1700, 1800 and 1900 were not leap years.

These tables follow the New Style from the date of its introduction by Pope Gregory in 1583, but should it be desired to express dates between that time and the year 1752, when the Gregorian calendar was adopted in England, ten days must be added to dates from 1583 to 1699 inclusive, and eleven days from that year to September 2, 1752.

TABLE I

Year of the Hijra.	Christian date of first day of the Hijra year.	Number of days of the Christian year elapsed.	Year of the Hijra.	Christian date of first day of the Hijra year.	Number of days of the Christian year elapsed.
1	622, July 16	196	34	654, July 22	202
2	623, July 5	185	35	655, July 11	191
3	*624, June 24	175	36	*656, June 30	181
4	625, June 13	163	37	657, June 19	169
5	626, June 2	152	38	658, June 9	159
6	627, May 23	141	39	659, May 29	148
7	*628, May 11	131	40	*660, May 17	137
8	629, May 1	120	41	661, May 7	126
9	630, April 20	109	42	662, April 26	115
10	631, April 9	98	43	663, April 15	104
11	*632, March 29	88	44	*664, April 4	94
12	633, March 18	76	45	665, March 24	82
13	634, March 7	65	46	666, March 13	71
14	635, February 25	55	47	667, March 3	61
15	*636, February 14	44	48	*668, February 20	50
16	637, February 2	32	49	669, February 9	39
17	638, January 23	22	50	670, January 29	28
18	639, January 12	11	51	671, January 18	17
19	*640, January 2	1	52	*672, January 8	7
20	*640, December 21	355	53	*672, December 27	361
21	641, December 10	343	54	673, December 16	349
22	642, November 30	333	55	674, December 6	339
23	643, November 19	322	56	675, November 25	328
24	*644, November 7	311	57	*676, November 14	318
25	645, October 28	300	58	677, November 3	306
26	646, October 17	289	59	678, October 23	295
27	647, October 7	279	60	679, October 13	285
28	*648, September 25	268	61	*680, October 1	274
29	649, September 14	256	62	681, September 20	262
30	650, September 4	246	63	682, September 10	252
31	651, August 24	235	64	683, August 30	241
32	*652, August 12	224	65	*684, August 18	230
33	653, August 2	213	66	685, August 8	219

TABLE I

Year of the Hijra.	Christian date of first day of the Hijra year.	Number of days of the Christian year elapsed.	Year of the Hijra.	Christian date of first day of the Hijra year.	Number of days of the Christian year elapsed.
67	686, July 28	208	102	*720, July 12	193
68	687, July 18	198	103	721, July 1	181
69	*688, July 6	187	104	722, June 21	171
70	689, June 25	175	105	723, June 10	160
71	690, June 15	165	106	*724, May 29	149
72	691, June 4	154	107	725, May 19	138
73	*692, May 23	143	108	726, May 8	127
74	693, May 13	132	109	727, April 28	117
75	694, May 2	121	110	*728, April 16	106
76	695, April 21	110	111	729, April 5	94
77	*696, April 10	100	112	730, March 26	84
78	697, March 30	88	113	731, March 15	73
79	698, March 20	78	114	*732, March 3	62
80	699, March 9	67	115	733, February 21	51
81	*700, February 26	56	116	734, February 10	40
82	701, February 15	45	117	735, January 31	30
83	702, February 4	34	118	*736, January 20	19
84	703, January 24	23	119	737, January 8	7
85	*704, January 14	13	120	737, December 29	362
86	705, January 2	1	121	738, December 18	351
87	705, December 23	356	122	739, December 7	340
88	706, December 12	345	123	*740, November 26	330
89	707, December 1	334	124	741, November 15	318
90	*708, November 20	324	125	742, November 4	307
91	709, November 9	312	126	743, October 25	297
92	710, October 29	301	127	*744, October 13	286
93	711, October 19	291	128	745, October 3	275
94	*712, October 7	280	129	746, September 22	264
95	713, September 26	268	130	747, September 11	253
96	714, September 16	258	131	*748, August 31	243
97	715, September 5	247	132	749, August 20	231
98	*716, August 25	237	133	750, August 9	220
99	717, August 14	225	134	751, July 30	210
100	718, August 3	214	135	*752, July 18	198
101	719, July 24	204	136	753, July 7	187

TABLE I

Year of the Hijra.	Christian date of first day of the Hijra year.	Number of days of the Christian year elapsed.	Year of the Hijra.	Christian date of first day of the Hijra year.	Number of days of the Christian year elapsed.
137	754, June 27	177	172	*788, June 11	162
138	755, June 16	166	173	789, May 31	150
139	*756, June 5	156	174	790, May 20	139
140	757, May 25	144	175	791, May 10	129
141	758, May 14	133	176	*792, April 28	118
142	759, May 4	123	177	793, April 18	107
143	*760, April 22	111	178	794, April 7	96
144	761, April 11	100	179	795, March 27	85
145	762, April 1	90	180	*796, March 16	75
146	763, March 21	79	181	797, March 5	63
147	*764, March 10	68	182	798, February 22	52
148	765, February 27	57	183	799, February 12	42
149	766, February 16	46	184	*800, February 1	31
150	767, February 6	36	185	801, January 20	19
151	*768, January 26	25	186	802, January 10	9
152	769, January 14	13	187	802, December 30	363
153	770, January 4	3	188	803, December 20	353
154	770, December 24	357	189	*804, December 8	342
155	771, December 13	346	190	805, November 27	330
156	*772, December 2	336	191	806, November 17	320
157	773, November 21	324	192	807, November 6	309
158	774, November 11	314	193	*808, October 25	298
159	775, October 31	303	194	809, October 15	287
160	*776, October 19	292	195	810, October 4	276
161	777, October 9	281	196	811, September 23	265
162	778, September 28	270	197	*812, September 12	255
163	779, September 17	259	198	813, September 1	243
164	*780, September 6	248	199	814, August 22	233
165	781, August 26	237	200	815, August 11	222
166	782, August 15	227	201	*816, July 30	211
167	783, August 5	216	202	817, July 20	200
168	*784, July 24	205	203	818, July 9	189
169	785, July 14	194	204	819, June 28	178
170	786, July 3	183	205	*820, June 17	168
171	787, June 22	172	206	821, June 6	156

TABLE I

Year of the Hijra.	Christian date of first day of the Hijra year.	Number of days of the Christian year elapsed.	Year of the Hijra.	Christian date of first day of the Hijra year.	Number of days of the Christian year elapsed.
207	822, May 27	146	242	*856, May 10	130
208	823, May 16	135	243	857, April 30	119
209	*824, May 4	123	244	858 April 19	108
210	825, April 24	113	245	859, April 8	97
211	826, April 13	102	246	*860, March 28	87
212	827, April 2	91	247	861, March 17	75
213	*828, March 22	81	248	862, March 7	65
214	829, March 11	69	249	863, February 24	54
215	830, February 25	58	250	*864, February 13	44
216	831, February 18	48	251	865, February 2	32
217	*832, February 7	37	252	866, January 22	21
218	833, January 27	26	253	867, January 11	10
219	834, January 16	15	254	*868, January 1	0
220	835, January 5	4	255	*868, December 20	353
221	*835, December 26	359	256	869, December 9	342
222	*836, December 14	347	257	870, November 29	332
223	837, December 3	336	258	871, November 18	321
224	838, November 23	326	259	*872, November 7	311
225	839, November 12	315	260	873, October 27	299
226	*840, October 31	304	261	874, October 16	288
227	841, October 21	293	262	875, October 6	278
228	842, October 10	282	263	*876, September 24	267
229	843, September 30	272	264	877, September 13	255
230	*844, September 18	261	265	878, September 3	245
231	845, September 7	249	266	879, August 23	234
232	846, August 28	239	267	*880, August 12	224
233	847, August 17	228	268	881, August 1	212
234	*848, August 5	216	269	882, July 21	201
235	849, July 26	206	270	883, July 11	191
236	850, July 15	195	271	*884, June 29	180
237	851, July 5	185	272	885, June 18	168
238	*852, June 23	174	273	886, June 8	158
239	853, June 12	162	274	887, May 28	147
240	854, June 2	152	275	*888, May 16	136
241	855, May 22	141	276	889, May 6	125

TABLE I

Year of the Hijra.	Christian date of first day of the Hijra year.	Number of days of the Christian year elapsed.	Year of the Hijra.	Christian date of first day of the Hijra year.	Number of days of the Christian year elapsed.
277	890, April 25	114	312	*924, April 9	99
278	891, April 15	104	313	925, March 29	87
279	*892, April 3	93	314	926, March 19	77
280	893, March 23	81	315	927, March 8	66
281	894, March 13	71	316	*928, February 25	55
282	895, March 2	60	317	929, February 14	44
283	*896, February 19	49	318	930, February 3	33
284	897, February 8	38	319	931, January 24	23
285	898, January 28	27	320	*932, January 13	12
286	899, January 17	16	321	933, January 1	0
287	*900, January 7	6	322	933, December 22	355
288	*900, December 26	360	323	934, December 11	344
289	901, December 16	349	324	935, November 30	333
290	902, December 5	338	325	*936, November 19	323
291	903, November 24	327	326	937, November 8	311
292	*904, November 13	317	327	938, October 29	301
293	905, November 2	305	328	939, October 18	291
294	906, October 22	294	329	*940, October 6	279
295	907, October 12	284	330	941, September 26	268
296	*908, September 30	273	331	942, September 15	257
297	909, September 20	262	332	943, September 4	246
298	910, September 9	251	333	*944, August 24	236
299	911, August 29	240	334	945, August 13	224
300	*912, August 18	230	335	946, August 2	213
301	913, August 7	218	336	947, July 23	203
302	914, July 27	207	337	*948, July 11	192
303	915, July 17	197	338	49, July 1	181
304	*916, July 5	186	339	950, June 20	170
305	917, June 24	174	340	951, June 9	159
306	918, June 14	164	341	*952, May 29	149
307	919, June 3	158	342	953, May 18	137
308	*920, May 23	143	343	954, May 7	126
309	921, May 12	131	344	955, April 27	116
310	922, May 1	120	345	*956, April 15	105
311	923, April 21	110	346	957, April 4	93

TABLE I

Year of the Hijra.	Christian date of first day of the Hijra year.	Number of days of the Christian year elapsed.	Year of the Hijra.	Christian date of first day of the Hijra year.	Number of days of the Christian year elapsed.
347	958, March 25	83	382	*992, March 9	68
348	959, March 14	72	383	993, February 26	56
349	*960, March 3	62	384	994, February 15	45
350	961, February 20	50	385	995, February 5	34
351	962, February 9	39	386	*996, February 25	24
352	963, January 30	29	387	997, January 14	13
353	*964, January 19	18	388	998, January 3	2
354	965, January 7	6	389	998, December 23	356
355	965, December 28	361	390	999, December 13	346
356	966, December 17	350	391	*1000, December 1	335
357	697, December 7	340	392	1001, November 20	323
358	*968, November 25	329	393	1002, November 10	313
359	969 November 14	317	394	1003, October 30	302
360	970, November 4	307	395	*1004, October 18	291
361	971, October 24	296	396	1005, October 8	281
362	*972, October 12	285	397	1006, September 27	269
363	973, October 2	274	398	1007, September 17	259
364	974, September 21	263	399	*1008, September 5	248
365	975, September 10	252	400	1009, August 25	236
366	*976, August 30	242	401	1010, August 15	226
367	977, August 19	231	402	1011, August 4	215
368	978, August 9	221	403	*1012, July 23	204
369	979, July 29	209	404	1013, July 13	193
370	*980, July 17	198	405	1014, July 3	183
371	981, July 7	187	406	1015, June 21	171
372	982, June 26	176	407	*1016, June 10	161
373	983, June 15	165	408	1017, May 30	149
374	*984, June 4	155	409	1018, May 20	139
375	985, May 24	143	410	1019, May 9	128
376	986, May 13	133	411	*1020, April 27	117
377	987, May 3	123	412	1021, April 17	106
378	*988, April 21	111	413	1022, April 6	95
379	989, April 11	100	414	1023, March 26	84
380	990, March 31	89	415	*1024, March 15	74
381	991, March 31	78	416	1025, March 4	62

TABLE I

Year of the Hijra.	Christian date of first day of the Hijra year.	Number of days of the Christian year elapsed.	Year of the Hijra.	Christian date of first day of the Hijra year.	Number of days of the Christian year elapsed.
417	1026, February 22	52	452	*1060, February 6	36
418	1027, February 11	41	453	1061, January 26	25
419	*1028, January 31	30	454	1062, January 15	14
420	1029, January 20	19	455	1063, January 4	3
421	1030, January 9	8	456	1063, December 25	358
422	1030, December 29	362	457	*1064, December 13	347
423	1031, December 19	352	458	1065, December 3	336
424	*1032, December 7	341	459	1066, November 22	325
425	1033, November 26	329	460	1067, November 11	314
426	1034, November 16	319	461	*1068, October 31	304
427	1035, November 5	308	462	1069, October 20	292
428	*1036, October 25	298	463	1070, October 9	281
429	1037, October 14	286	464	1071, September 29	271
430	1038, October 3	275	465	*1072, September 17	269
431	1039, September 23	265	466	1073, September 6	248
432	*1040, September 11	254	467	1074, August 27	238
433	1041, August 31	242	468	1075, August 16	227
434	1042, August 21	232	469	*1076, August 5	217
435	1043, August 10	221	470	1077, July 25	205
436	*1044, July 29	210	471	1078, July 14	194
437	1045, July 19	199	472	1079, July 4	184
438	1046, July 8	188	473	*1080, June 22	173
439	1047. June 28	178	474	1081, June 11	161
440	*1048, June 16	167	475	1082, June 1	151
441	1049, June 5	155	476	1083, May 21	140
442	1050, May 26	145	477	*1084, May 10	130
443	1051, May 15	134	478	1085, April 29	118
444	*1052, May 3	123	479	1086, April 18	107
445	1053, April 23	112	480	1087, April 8	97
446	1054, April 12	101	481	*1088, March 27	86
447	1055, April 2	91	482	1089, March 16	74
448	*1056, March 21	80	483	1090, March 6	64
449	1057, March 10	68	484	1091, February 23	53
450	1058, February 28	58	485	*1092, February 12	42
451	1059, February 17	47	486	1093, February 1	31

TABLE I

Year of the Hijra.	Christian date of first day of the Hijra year.	Number of days of the Christian year elapsed.	Year of the Hijra.	Christian date of first day of the Hijra year.	Number of days of the Christian year elapsed.
487	1094, January 21	20	522	*1128, January 6	5
488	1095, January 11	10	523	*1128, December 25	359
489	1095, December 31	364	524	1129, December 15	348
490	*1096, December 19	353	525	1130, December 4	337
491	1097, December 9	342	526	1131, November 23	326
492	1098, November 28	331	527	*1132, November 12	316
493	1099, November 17	320	528	1133, November 1	304
494	*1100, November 6	310	529	1134, October 22	294
495	1101, October 26	298	530	1135, October 11	283
496	1102, October 15	287	531	*1136, September 29	272
497	1103, October 5	277	532	1137, September 19	261
498	*1104, September 23	265	533	1138, September 8	250
499	1105, September 13	255	534	1139, August 28	239
500	1106, September 2	244	535	*1140, August 17	229
501	1107, August 22	233	536	1141, August 6	217
502	*1108, August 11	223	537	1142, July 27	207
503	1109, July 31	211	538	1143, July 16	196
504	1110, July 20	200	539	*1144, July 4	185
505	1111, July 10	190	540	1145, June 24	174
506	*1112, June 28	179	541	1146, June 13	163
507	1113, June 18	168	542	1147, June 2	152
508	1114, June 7	157	543	*1148, May 22	142
509	1115, May 27	146	544	1149, May 11	130
510	*1116, May 16	136	545	1150, April 30	119
511	1117, May 5	124	546	1151, April 20	109
512	1118, April 24	113	547	*1152, April 8	98
513	1119, April 14	103	548	1153, March 27	87
514	*1120, April 2	92	549	1154, March 18	76
515	1121, March 22	80	550	1155, March 7	65
516	1122, March 12	70	551	*1156, February 25	55
517	1123, March 1	59	552	1157, February 13	43
518	*1124, February 19	49	553	1158, February 2	32
519	1125, February 7	37	554	1159, Janyary 23	22
520	1126, January 27	26	555	*1160, January 12	11
521	1127, January 17	16	556	*1160, December 31	365

TABLE I

Year of the Hijra.	Christian date of first day of the Hijra year.	Number of days of the Christian year elapsed.	Year of the Hijra.	Christian date of first day of the Hijra year.	Number of days of the Christian year elapsed.
557	1161, December 21	354	592	1195, December 6	339
558	1162, December 10	343	593	*1196, November 24	328
559	1163, November 30	333	594	1197, November 13	316
560	*1164, November 18	322	595	1198, November 3	306
561	1165, November 7	310	596	1199, October 23	295
562	1166, October 28	300	597	*1200, October 12	285
563	1167, October 17	289	598	1201, October 1	274
564	*1168, October 5	278	599	1202, September 20	262
565	1169, September 25	267	600	1203, September 10	252
566	1170, September 14	256	601	*1204, August 29	231
567	1171, September 4	246	602	1205, August 18	229
568	*1172, August 23	235	603	1206, August 8	219
569	1173, August 12	223	604	1207, July 28	208
570	1174, August 2	213	605	*1208, July 16	197
571	1175, July 22	202	606	1209, July 6	186
572	*1176, July 10	191	607	1210, June 25	175
573	1177, June 30	180	608	1211, June 15	166
574	1178, June 19	169	609	*1212, June 3	154
575	1179, June 8	158	610	1213, May 23	142
576	*1180, May 28	147	611	1214, May 13	132
577	1181, May 17	136	612	1215, May 2	121
578	1182, May 7	126	613	*1216, April 20	110
579	1183, April 26	115	614	1217, April 10	99
580	*1184, April 14	104	615	1218, March 30	88
581	1185, April 4	93	616	1219, March 19	77
582	1186, March 24	82	617	*1220, March 8	67
583	1187, March 13	71	618	1221, February 25	55
584	*1188, March 2	61	619	1222, February 15	45
585	1189, February 19	49	620	1223, February 4	34
586	1190, February 8	38	621	*1224, January 24	23
587	1191, January 29	28	622	1225, January 13	12
588	*1192, January 18	17	623	1226, January 2	1
589	1193, January 7	6	624	1226, December 22	355
590	1193, December 27	360	625	1227, December 12	345
591	1194, December 16	349	626	*1228, November 30	334

TABLE I

Year of the Hijra.	Christian date of first day of the Hijra year.	Number of days of the Christian year elapsed.	Year of the Hijra.	Christian date of first day of the Hijra year.	Number of days of the Christian year elapsed.
627	1229, November 20	323	662	1263, November 4	307
628	1230, November 9	312	663	*1264, October 24	297
629	1231, October 29	301	664	1265, October 13	285
630	*1232, October 18	291	665	1266, October 2	274
631	1233, October 7	279	666	1267, September 22	264
632	1234, September 25	268	667	*1268, September 10	253
633	1235, September 16	258	668	1269, August 31	242
634	*1236, September 4	247	669	1270, August 20	231
635	1237, August 24	235	670	1271, August 9	220
636	1238, August 14	225	671	*1272, July 29	210
637	1239, August 3	214	672	1273, July 18	198
638	*1240, July 23	203	673	1274, July 7	187
639	1241, July 12	192	674	1275, June 27	177
640	1242, July 1	181	675	*1276, June 15	166
641	1243, June 21	171	676	1277, June 4	155
642	*1244, June 9	160	677	1278, May 25	144
643	1245, May 29	248	678	1279, May 14	133
644	1246, May 19	138	679	*1280, May 3	123
645	1247, May 8	127	680	1281, April 22	111
646	*1248, April 26	116	681	1282, April 11	100
647	1249, April 16	105	682	1283, April 1	90
648	1250, April 5	94	683	*1284, March 20	79
649	1251, March 26	85	684	1285, March 9	67
650	*1252, March 14	73	685	1286, February 27	57
651	1253, March 3	61	686	1287, February 16	46
652	1254, February 21	51	687	*1288, February 6	36
653	1255, February 10	40	688	1289, January 25	24
654	*1256, January 30	29	689	1290, January 14	13
655	1257, January 19	18	690	1291, January 4	3
656	1258, January 8	7	691	1291, December 24	357
657	1258, December 29	362	692	*1292, December 12	346
658	1259, December 18	351	693	1293, December 2	335
659	*1260, December 6	340	694	1294, November 21	324
660	1261, November 26	329	695	1295, November 10	313
661	1262, November 15	318	696	*1296, October 30	303

TABLE I

Year of the Hijra.	Christian date of first day of the Hijra year.	Number of days of the Christian year elapsed.	Year of the Hijra.	Christian date of first day of the Hijra year.	Number of days of the Christian year elapsed.
697	1297, October 19	291	732	1331, October 4	276
698	1298, October 9	281	733	*1332, September 22	265
699	1299, September 28	270	734	1333, September 12	254
700	*1300, September 16	259	735	1334, September 1	243
701	1301, September 5	248	736	1335, August 21	232
702	1302, August 26	237	737	*1336, August 10	222
703	1303, August 15	226	738	1337, July 30	210
704	*1304, August 4	216	739	1338, July 20	200
705	1305, July 24	204	740	1339, July 9	189
706	1306, July 13	193	741	*1340, June 27	178
707	1307, July 3	183	742	1341, June 17	167
708	*1308, June 21	172	743	1342, June 6	156
709	1309, June 11	161	744	1343, May 26	145
710	1310, May 31	150	745	*1344, May 15	135
711	1311, May 20	139	746	1345, May 4	123
712	*1312, May 9	129	747	1346, April 24	113
713	1313, April 28	117	748	1347, April 13	102
714	1314, April 17	106	749	*1348, April 1	91
715	1315, April 7	96	750	1349, March 22	80
716	*1316, March 26	85	751	1350, March 11	69
717	1317, March 16	74	752	1351, February 28	58
718	1318, March 5	63	753	*1352, February 18	48
719	1319, February 22	52	754	1353, February 6	36
720	*1320, February 12	42	755	1354, January 26	25
721	1321, January 31	30	756	1355, January 16	15
722	1322, January 20	19	757	*1356, January 5	4
723	1323, January 10	9	758	*1356, December 25	359
724	1323, December 30	363	759	1357, December 15	347
725	*1324, December 18	352	760	1358, December 3	336
726	1325, December 8	341	761	1359, November 23	326
727	1326, November 27	330	762	*1360, November 11	315
728	1327, November 17	320	763	1361, October 31	303
729	*1328, November 5	309	764	1362, October 21	293
730	1329, October 25	297	765	1363, October 10	282
731	1330, October 15	287	766	*1364, September 28	271

TABLE I

Year of the Hijra.	Christian date of first day of the Hijra year.	Number of days of the Christian year elapsed.	Year of the Hijra.	Christian date of first day of the Hijra year.	Number of days of the Christian year elapsed.
767	1365, September 18	260	802	1399, September 3	245
768	1366, September 7	249	803	*1400, August 22	234
769	1367, August 28	239	804	1401, August 11	222
770	*1368, August 16	228	805	1402, August 1	212
771	1369, August 5	216	806	1403, July 21	201
772	1370, July 26	206	807	*1404, July 10	191
773	1371, July 15	195	808	1405, June 29	179
774	*1372, July 3	184	809	1406, June 18	168
775	1373, June 23	173	810	1407, June 8	158
776	1374, June 12	162	811	*1408, May 27	147
777	1375, June 2	152	812	1409, May 16	136
778	*1376, May 21	141	813	1410, May 6	126
779	1377, May 10	129	814	1411, April 25	114
780	1378, April 30	119	815	*1412, April 13	103
781	1379, April 19	109	816	1413, April 3	92
782	*1380, April 7	97	817	1414, March 23	81
783	1381, March 28	86	818	1415, March 13	71
784	1382, March 17	75	819	*1416, March 1	60
785	1383, March 6	64	820	1417, February 18	48
786	*1384, February 24	54	821	1418, February 8	38
787	1385, February 12	42	822	1419, January 28	27
788	1386, February 2	32	823	*1420, January17	16
789	1387, January 22	21	824	1421, January 6	5
790	*1388, January 11	10	825	1421, December 26	359
791	*1388, December 31	365	826	1422, December 15	348
792	1389, December 20	353	827	1423, December 5	338
793	1390, December 9	342	828	*1424, November 23	327
794	1391, November 29	332	829	1425, November 13	316
795	*1392, November 17	321	830	1426, November 2	305
796	1393, November 6	309	831	1427, October 22	294
797	1394, October 27	299	832	*1428, October 11	284
798	1395, October 16	288	833	1429, September 30	272
799	*1396, October 5	278	834	1430, September 19	261
800	1397, September 24	266	835	1431, September 9	251
801	1398, September 13	255	836	*1432, August 28	240

TABLE I

Year of the Hijra.	Christian date of first day of the Hijra year.	Number of days of the Christian year elapsed.	Year of the Hijra.	Christian date of first day of the Hijra year.	Number of days of the Christian year elapsed.
837	1433, August 18	229	873	*1468, July 22	203
838	1434, August 7	218	874	1469, July 11	191
839	1435, July 27	207	875	1470, June 30	180
840	*1436, July 16	197	876	1471, June 20	170
841	1437, July 5	185	877	*1472, June 8	159
842	1438, June 24	174	878	1473, May 29	148
843	1439, June 14	164	879	1474, May 18	137
844	*1440, June 2	153	880	1475, May 7	126
845	1441, May 22	141	881	*1476, April 26	116
846	1442, May 12	131	882	1477, April 15	104
847	1443, May 1	120	883	1478, April 4	93
848	*1444, April 20	110	884	1479, March 25	83
849	1445, April 9	98	885	*1480, March 13	72
850	1446, March 29	87	886	1481, March 2	60
851	1447, March 19	77	887	1482, February 20	50
852	*1448, March 7	66	888	1483, February 9	39
853	1449, February 24	54	889	*1484, January 30	29
854	1450, February 14	44	890	1485, January 18	17
855	1451, February 3	33	891	1486, January 7	6
856	*1452, January 23	22	892	1486, December 28	361
857	1453, January 12	11	893	1487, December 17	350
858	1454, January 1	0	894	*1488, December 5	339
859	1454, December 22	355	895	1489, November 25	328
860	1455, December 11	344	896	1490, November 14	317
861	*1456, November 29	333	897	1491, November 4	307
862	1457, November 19	322	898	*1492, October 23	296
863	1458, November 8	311	899	1493, October 12	284
864	1459, October 28	300	900	1494, October 2	274
865	*1460, October 17	290	901	1495, September 21	263
866	1461, October 6	278	902	*1496, September 9	252
867	1462, September 26	268	903	1497, August 30	241
868	1463, September 15	257	904	1498, August 19	230
869	*1464, September 3	246	905	1499, August 8	219
870	1465, August 23	234	906	*1500, July 28	209
871	1466, August 13	224	907	1501, July 17	197
872	1467, August 2	213			

TABLE I

Year of the Hijra.	Christian date of first day of the Hijra year.	Number of days of the Christian year clapsed.	Year of the Hijra.	Christian date of first day of the Hijra year.	Number of days of the Christian year elapsed.
908	1502, July 7	188	943	*1536, June 20	171
909	1503, June 26	176	944	1537, June 10	161
910	*1504, June 14	165	945	1538, May 30	149
911	1505, June 4	154	946	1539, May 19	138
912	1506, May 24	143	947	*1540, May 8	128
913	1507, May 13	132	948	1541, April 27	116
914	*1508, May 2	122	949	1542, April 17	106
915	1509, April 21	110	950	1543, April 6	95
916	1510, April 10	99	951	*1544, March 25	84
917	1511, March 31	89	952	1545, March 15	73
918	*1512, March 19	78	953	1546, March 4	62
919	1513, March 9	67	954	1547, February 21	51
920	1514, February 26	56	955	*1548, February 11	41
921	1515, February 15	46	956	1549, January 30	29
922	*1516, February 5	35	957	1550, January 20	19
923	1517, January 24	23	958	1551, January 9	8
924	1518, January 13	12	959	1551, December 29	362
925	1519, January 3	2	960	*1552, December 18	352
926	1519 December 23	356	961	1553, December 7	340
927	*1520, December 12	346	962	1554. November 26	329
928	1521. December 1	334	963	1555, November 16	319
929	1522. November 20	323	964	*1556, November 4	308
930	1523 November 10	313	965	1557, October 24	296
331	*1524 October 29	302	966	1558, October 14	286
932	1525, October 18	290	967	1559, October 3	275
933	1526, October 8	280	968	*1560, September 22	265
934	1527. September 27	269	969	1561, September 11	253
935	*1528, September 15	258	970	1562, August 31	242
936	1529, September 5	247	971	1563, August 21	232
937	1530, August 25	236	972	*1564, August 9	221
938	1531, August 15	226	973	1565, July 29	209
939	*1532. August 3	215	974	1566, July 19	199
940	1533, July 23	203	975	1567, July 8	188
941	1534, July 13	193	976	*1568, June 26	177
942	1535, July 2	182	977	1569, June 16	166

TABLE I

Year of the Hijra.	Christian date of first day of the Hijra year.	Number of days of the Christian year elapsed.	Year of the Hijra.	Christian date of first day of the Hijra year.	Number of days of the Christian year elapsed.
978	1570, June 5	155	1010	1601, July 2	182
979	1571, May 26	145	1011	1602, June 21	171
980	*1572, May 14	134	1012	1603, June 11	161
981	1573, May 3	122	1013	*1604, May 30	150
982	1574, April 23	112	1014	1605, May 19	138
983	1575, April 12	101	1015	1606, May 9	128
984	*1576, March 31	90	1016	1607, April 28	117
985	1577, March 21	79	1017	*1608, April 17	107
986	1578, March 10	68	1018	1609, April 6	95
987	1579, February 28	58	1019	1610, March 26	84
988	*1580, February 17	47	1020	1611, March 16	74
989	1581, February 5	35	1021	*1612, March 4	63
990	1582, January 26	25	1022	1613, February 21	51
991	1583, January 25†	24	1023	1614, February 11	41
992	*1584, January 14	13	1024	1615, January 31	30
993	1585, January 3	2	1025	*1616, January 20	19
994	1585, December 23	356	1026	1617, January 9	8
995	1586, December 12	345	1027	1617, December 29	362
996	1587, December 2	335	1028	1618, December 19	352
997	*1588, November 20	324	1029	1619, December 8	341
998	1589, November 10	313	1030	*1620, November 26	330
999	1590, October 30	302	1031	1621, November 16	319
1000	1591, October 19	291	1032	1622, November 5	308
1001	*1592, October 8	281	1033	1623, October 25	297
1002	1593, September 27	269	1034	*1624, October 14	287
1003	1594, September 16	258	1035	1625, October 3	275
1004	1595, September 6	248	1036	1626, September 22	264
1005	*1596, August 28	237	1037	1627, September 12	254
1006	1597, August 14	225	1038	*1628, August 31	243
1007	1598, August 4	215	1039	1629, August 21	232
1008	1599, July 24	204	1040	1630, August 10	221
1009	*1600, July 13	194	1041	1631, July 30	210

†In 1582, Pope Gregory XIII corrected the Julian Calendar and from 1583 onwards Christian dates are given in the New, or Gregorian Style. If it be desired to alter them to the Old, or Julian Style, which was in use in England until 1752, ten days must be added to dates from 1583 to 1699 inclusive and eleven days from 1699 to September 2, 1752.

TABLE I

Year of the Hijra.	Christian date of first day of the Hijra year.	Number of days of the Christian year elapsed.	Year of the Hijra.	Christian date of first day of the Hijra year.	Number of days of the Christian year elapsed.
1042	*1632, July 19	200	1077	1666, July 4	184
1043	1633, July 8	188	1078	1667, June 23	173
1044	1634, June 27	177	1079	*1668, June 11	162
1045	1635, June 17	167	1080	1669, June 1	151
1046	*1636, June 5	156	1081	1670, May 21	140
1047	1637, May 26	145	1082	1671, May 10	129
1048	1638, May 15	134	1083	*1672, April 29	119
1049	1639, May 4	123	1084	1673, April 18	107
1050	*1640, April 23	113	1085	1674, April 7	96
1051	1641, April 12	101	1086	1675, March 28	86
1052	1642, April 1	90	1087	*1676, March 16	75
1053	1643, March 22	80	1088	1677, March 6	64
1054	*1644, March 10	69	1089	1678, February 23	53
1055	1645, February 27	57	1090	1679, February 12	42
1056	1646, February 17	47	1091	*1680, February 2	32
1057	1647, February 6	36	1092	1681, January 21	20
1058	*1648, January 27	26	1093	1682, January 10	9
1059	1649, January 15	14	1094	1682, December 31	364
1060	1650, January 4	3	1095	1683, December 20	353
1061	1650, December 25	358	1096	*1684, December 8	342
1062	1651, December 14	347	1097	1685, November 28	331
1063	*1652, December 2	336	1098	1686, November 17	320
1064	1653, November 22	325	1099	1687, November 7	310
1065	1654, November 11	314	1100	*1688, October 26	299
1066	1655, October 31	303	1101	1689, October 15	287
1067	*1656, October 20	293	1102	1690, October 5	277
1068	1657, October 9	281	1103	1691, September 24	266
1069	1658, September 29	271	1104	*1692, September 12	255
1070	1659, September 18	260	1105	1693, September 2	244
1071	*1660, September 6	249	1106	1694, August 22	233
1072	1661, August 27	238	1107	1695, August 12	223
1073	1662, August 16	227	1108	*1696, July 31	212
1074	1663, August 5	216	1109	1697, July 20	200
1075	*1664, July 25	206	1110	1698, July 10	190
1076	1665, July 14	194	1111	1699, June 29	179

TABLE I

Year of the Hijra.	Christian date of first day of the Hijra year.	Number of days of the Christian year elapsed.	Year of the Hijra.	Christian date of first day of the Hijra year.	Number of days of the Christian year elapsed.
1112	1700, June 18	168	1147	1734, June 3	153
1113	1701, June 8	158	1148	1735, May 24	143
1114	1702, May 28	147	1149	*1736, May 12	132
1115	1703, May 17	136	1150	1737, May 1	120
1116	*1704, May 6	125	1151	1738, April 21	110
1117	1705, April 25	114	1152	1739, April 10	99
1118	1706, April 15	104	1153	*1740, March 29	88
1119	1707, April 4	93	1154	1741, March 19	77
1120	*1708, March 23	82	1155	1742, March 8	66
1121	1709, March 13	71	1156	1743, February 25	55
1122	1710, March 2	60	1157	*1744, February 15	45
1123	1711, February 19	49	1158	1745, February 3	33
1124	*1712, February 9	39	1159	1746, January 24	23
1125	1713, January 28	27	1160	1747, January 13	12
1126	1714, January 17	16	1161	*1748, January 2	1
1127	1715, January 7	6	1162	*1748, December 22	356
1128	1715, December 27	360	1163	1749, December 11	334
1129	*1716, December 16	350	1164	1750, November 30	333
1130	1717, December 5	308	1165	1751, November 20	323
1131	1718, November 24	327	1166	*1752, November 8	312
1132	1719, November 14	317	1167	1753, October 29	301
1133	*1720, November 2	306	1168	1754, October 18	290
1134	1721, October 22	294	1169	1755, October 7	279
1135	1722, October 12	284	1170	*1756, September 26	269
1136	1723, October 1	273	1171	1757, September 15	257
1137	*1724, September 20	263	1172	1758, September 4	246
1138	1725, September 9	251	1173	1759, August 25	236
1139	1726, August 29	240	1174	*1760, August 13	215
1140	1727, August 19	230	1175	1761, August 2	213
1141	*1728, August 7	219	1176	1762, July 23	203
1142	1729, July 27	207	1177	1763, July 12	192
1143	1730, July 17	197	1178	*1764, July 1	182
1144	1731, July 6	186	1179	1765, June 20	170
1145	*1732, June 24	175	1180	1766, June 9	159
1146	1733, June 14	164	1181	1767, May 30	149

TABLE I

Year of the Hijra.	Christian date of first day of the Hijra year.	Number of days of the Christian year elapsed.	Year of the Hijra.	Christian date of first day of the Hijra year.	Number of days of the Christian year elapsed.
1182	*1768, May 18	138	1217	1802, May 4	123
1183	1769, May 7	126	1218	1803, April 23	112
1184	1770, April 27	116	1219	*1804, April 12	102
1185	1771, April 16	105	1220	1805, April 1	90
1186	*1772, April 4	94	1221	1806, March 21	79
1187	1773, March 25	83	1222	1807, March 11	69
1188	1774, March 14	72	1223	*1808, February 28	58
1189	1775, March 4	62	1224	1809, February 16	46
1190	*1776, February 21	51	1225	1810, February 6	36
1191	1777, February 19	39	1226	1811, January 26	25
1192	1778, January 30	29	1227	1812, January 16	15
1193	1779, January 19	18	1228	1813, January 4	3
1194	*1780, January 8	7	1229	1813, December 24	357
1195	*1780, December 28	362	1230	1814, December 14	347
1196	1781, December 17	350	1231	1815, December 3	336
1197	1782, December 7	340	1232	*1816, November 21	325
1198	1783, November 26	329	1233	1817, November 11	314
1199	*1784, November 14	318	1234	1818, October 31	303
1200	1785, November 4	307	1235	1819, October 20	292
1201	1786, October 24	296	1236	*1820, October 9	282
1202	1784, October 13	285	1237	1821, September 28	270
1203	*1788, October 2	275	1238	1822, September 18	260
1204	1789, September 21	263	1239	1823, September 7	249
1205	1790, September 10	252	1240	*1824, August 26	238
1206	1791, August 31	242	1241	1825, August 16	227
1207	*1792, August 19	231	1242	1826, August 5	216
1208	1793, August 9	220	1243	1827, July 25	205
1209	1794, July 29	209	1244	*1828, July 14	195
1210	1795, July 18	198	1245	1829, July 3	183
1211	*1796, July 7	188	1246	1830, June 22	172
1212	1797, June 26	176	1247	1831, June 12	162
1213	1798, June 15	165	1248	*1832, May 31	151
1214	1799, June 5	155	1249	1833, May 21	140
1215	1800, May 25	144	1250	1834, May 10	129
1216	1801, May 14	133	1251	*1835, April 29	118

TABLE I

Year of the Hijra.	Christian date of first day of the Hijra year.	Number of days of the Christian year elapsed.	Year of the Hijra.	Christian date of first day of the Hijra year.	Number of days of the Christian year elapsed.
1252	*1836, April 18	108	1287	1870, April 3	92
1253	1837, April 7	96	1288	1871, March 23	81
1254	1838, March 27	85	1289	*1872, March 11	70
1255	1839, March 17	75	1290	1873, March 1	59
1256	*1840, March 5	64	1291	1874, February 18	48
1257	1841, February 23	53	1292	1875, February 7	37
1258	1842, February 12	42	1293	*1876, January 28	27
1259	1843, February 1	31	1294	1877, January 16	15
1260	*1844, January 22	21	1295	1878, January 5	4
1261	1845, January 10	9	1296	1878, December 26	359
1262	1845, December 30	363	1297	1879, December 15	348
1263	1846, December 20	353	1298	*1880, December 4	338
1264	1847, December 9	342	1299	1881, November 23	326
1265	*1848, November 27	331	1300	1882, November 12	315
1266	1849, November 17	320	1301	1883, November 2	305
1267	1850, November 6	309	1302	*1884, October 21	294
1268	1851, October 27	299	1303	1885, October 10	282
1269	*1852, October 15	288	1304	1886, September 30	272
1270	1853, October 4	276	1305	1887, September 19	261
1271	1854, September 24	266	1306	*1888, September 7	250
1272	1855, September 13	255	1307	1889, August 28	239
1273	*1856, September 1	244	1308	1890, August 17	228
1274	1857, August 22	233	1309	1891, August 7	218
1275	1858, August 11	222	1310	*1892, July 26	207
1276	1859, July 31	211	1311	1893, July 15	195
1277	*1860, July 20	201	1312	1894, July 5	185
1278	1861, July 9	189	1313	1895, June 24	174
1279	1862, June 29	179	1314	*1896, June 12	163
1280	1863, June 18	168	1315	1897, June 2	152
1281	*1864, June 6	157	1316	1898, May 22	141
1282	1865, May 27	146	1317	1899, May 12	131
1283	1866, May 16	135	1318	*1900, May 1	120
1284	1867, May 5	124	1319	1901, April 20	109
1285	*1868, April 24	114	1320	1902, April 10	99
1286	1869, April 13	102	1321	1903, March 30	88

TABLE I

Year of the Hijra.	Christian date of first day of the Hijra year.	Number of days of the Christian year elapsed.	Year of the Hijra.	Christian date of first day of the Hijra year.	Number of days of the Christian year elapsed.
1322	*1904, March 18	77	1357	1938, March 3	61
1323	1905, March 8	66	1358	1939, February 21	51
1324	1906, February 25	55	1359	*1940, February 10	40
1325	1907, February 14	44	1360	1941, January 29	28
1326	*1908, February 4	34	1361	1942, January 19	18
1327	1909, January 23	22	1362	1943, January 8	7
1328	1910, January 13	12	1363	1943, December 28	361
1329	1911, January 2	1	1364	*1944, December 17	351
1330	1911, December 22	355	1365	1945, December 6	339
1331	*1912, December 11	345	1366	1946, November 25	328
1332	1913, November 30	333	1367	1947, November 15	318
1333	1914, November 19	322	1368	*1948, November 3	307
1334	1915, November 9	312	1369	1949, October 24	296
1335	*1916, October 28	301	1370	1950, October 13	285
1336	1917, October 17	289	1371	1951, October 2	274
1337	1918, October 7	279	1372	*1952, September 21	264
1338	1919, September 26	268	1373	1953, September 10	252
1339	*1920, September 15	258	1374	1954, August 30	241
1340	1921, September 4	246	1375	1955, August 20	231
1341	1922, August 24	235	1376	*1956, August 8	220
1342	1923, August 14	255	1377	1957, July 29	209
1343	*1924, August 2	214	1378	1958, July 18	198
1344	1925, July 22	202	1379	1959, July 7	187
1345	1926, July 12	192	1380	*1960, June 26	177
1346	1927, July 1	181	1381	1961, June 15	165
1347	*1928, June 20	171	1382	1962, June 4	154
1348	1929, June 9	159	1383	1963, May 25	144
1349	1930, May 29	148	1384	*1964, May 13	133
1350	1931, May 19	138	1385	1965, May 2	121
1351	*1932, May 7	127	1386	1966, April 22	111
1352	1933, April 26	115	1387	1967, April 11	100
1353	1934, April 16	105	1388	*1968, March 31	90
1354	1935, April 5	94	1389	1969, March 20	78
1355	*1936, March 24	83	1390	1970, March 9	67
1356	1937, March 14	72	1391	1971, February 27	57

TABLE I

Year of the Hijra.	Christian date of first day of the Hijra year.	Number of days of the Christian year elapsed.	Year of the Hijra.	Christian date of first day of the Hijra year.	Number of days of the Christian year elapsed.
1392	*1972, February 16	46	1407	1986, September 6	248
1393	1973, February 4	34	1408	1987, August 26	237
1394	1974, January 25	24	1409	*1988, August 14	226
1395	1975, January 14	13	1410	1989, August 4	215
1396	*1976, January 3	2	1411	1990, July 24	204
1397	*1976, December 23	357	1412	1991, July 13	193
1398	1977, December 12	345	1413	*1992, July 2	183
1399	1978, December 2	335	1414	1993, June 21	171
1400	1979, November 21	324	1415	1994, June 10	160
1401	*1980, November 9	313	1416	1995, May 31	150
1402	1981, October 30	302	1417	*1996, May 19	139
1403	1982, October 19	291	1418	1997, May 9	128
1404	1983, October 8	280	1419	1998, April 28	117
1405	*1984, September 27	270	1420	1999, April 17	106
1406	1985, September 16	258	1421	*2000, April 6	96

TABLE II

JANUARY.			FEBRUARY.			MARCH.			APRIL.		
Year.		Day of the year	Year.		Day of the year	Year.		Day of the year	Year.		Day of the year
Common	Leap		Common	Leap		Common	Leap		Common	Leap	
1	1	1	1	1	32	1	—	60	1	—	91
2	2	2	2	2	33	2	1	61	2	1	92
3	3	3	3	3	34	3	2	62	3	2	93
4	4	4	4	4	35	4	3	63	4	3	94
5	5	5	5	5	36	5	4	64	5	4	95
6	6	6	6	6	37	6	5	65	6	5	96
7	7	7	7	7	38	7	6	66	7	6	97
8	8	8	8	8	39	8	7	67	8	7	98
9	9	9	9	9	40	9	8	68	9	8	99
10	10	10	10	10	41	10	9	69	10	9	100
11	11	11	11	11	42	11	10	70	11	10	101
12	12	12	12	12	43	12	11	71	12	11	102
13	13	13	13	13	44	13	12	72	13	12	103
14	14	14	14	14	45	14	13	73	14	13	104
15	15	15	15	15	46	15	14	74	15	14	105
16	16	16	16	16	47	16	15	75	16	15	106
17	17	17	17	17	48	17	16	76	17	16	107
18	18	18	18	18	49	18	17	77	18	17	108
19	19	19	19	19	50	19	18	78	19	18	109
20	20	20	20	20	51	20	19	79	20	19	110
21	21	21	21	21	52	21	20	80	21	20	111
22	22	22	22	22	53	22	21	81	22	21	112
23	23	23	23	23	54	23	22	82	23	22	113
24	24	24	24	24	55	24	23	83	24	23	114
25	25	25	25	25	56	25	24	84	25	24	115
26	26	26	26	26	57	26	25	85	26	25	116
27	27	27	27	27	58	27	26	86	27	26	117
28	28	28	28	28	59	28	27	87	28	27	118
29	29	29	—	29	60	29	28	88	29	28	119
30	30	30	—	—	—	30	29	89	30	29	120
31	31	31	—	—	—	31	30	90	—	30	121
—	—	—	—	—	—	—	31	91	—	—	—

TABLE II

MAY.			JUNE.			JULY.			AUGUST.		
Year.		Day of the year	Year.		Day of the year	Year.		Day of the year	Year.		Day of the year
Common	Leap		Common	Leap		Common	Leap		Common	Leap	
1	—	121	1	—	152	1	—	182	1	—	213
2	1	122	2	1	153	2	1	183	2	1	214
3	2	123	3	2	154	3	2	184	3	2	215
4	3	124	4	3	155	4	3	185	4	3	216
5	4	125	5	4	156	5	4	186	5	4	217
6	5	126	6	5	157	6	5	187	6	5	218
7	6	127	7	6	158	7	6	188	7	6	219
8	7	128	8	7	159	8	7	189	8	7	220
9	8	129	9	8	160	9	8	190	9	8	221
10	9	130	10	9	161	10	9	191	10	9	222
11	10	131	11	10	162	11	10	192	11	10	223
12	11	132	12	11	163	12	11	193	12	11	224
13	12	133	13	12	164	13	12	194	13	12	225
14	13	134	14	13	165	14	13	195	14	13	226
15	14	135	15	14	166	15	14	196	15	14	227
16	15	136	16	15	167	16	15	197	16	15	228
17	16	137	17	16	168	17	16	198	17	16	229
18	17	138	18	17	169	18	17	199	18	17	230
19	18	139	19	18	170	19	18	200	19	18	231
20	19	140	20	19	171	20	19	201	20	19	232
21	20	141	21	20	172	21	20	202	21	20	233
22	21	142	22	21	173	22	21	203	22	21	234
23	22	143	23	22	174	23	22	204	23	22	235
24	23	144	24	23	175	24	23	205	24	23	236
25	24	145	25	24	176	25	24	206	25	24	237
26	25	146	26	25	177	26	25	207	26	25	238
27	26	147	27	26	178	27	26	208	27	26	239
28	27	148	28	27	179	28	27	209	28	27	240
29	28	149	29	28	180	29	28	210	29	28	241
30	29	150	30	29	181	30	29	211	30	29	242
31	30	151	—	30	182	31	30	212	31	30	243
—	31	152	—	—	—	—	31	213	—	31	244

TABLE II

SEPTEMBER.			OCTOBER.			NOVEMBER.			DECEMBER.		
Year.		Day of the year	Year.		Day of the year	Year.		Day of the year	Year.		Day of the year
Common	Leap		Common	Leap		Common	Leap		Common	Leap	
1	—	244	1	—	274	1	—	305	1	—	335
2	1	245	2	1	275	2	1	306	2	1	236
3	2	246	3	2	276	3	2	307	3	2	337
4	3	247	4	3	277	4	3	308	4	3	338
5	4	248	5	4	278	5	4	309	5	4	339
6	5	249	6	5	279	6	5	310	6	5	340
7	6	250	7	6	280	7	6	311	7	6	341
8	7	251	8	7	281	8	7	312	8	7	342
9	8	252	9	8	282	9	8	313	9	8	343
10	9	253	10	9	283	10	9	314	10	9	344
11	10	254	11	10	284	11	10	315	11	10	345
12	11	255	12	11	285	12	11	316	12	11	346
13	12	256	13	12	286	13	12	317	13	12	347
14	13	257	14	13	287	14	13	318	14	13	348
15	14	258	15	14	288	15	14	319	15	14	349
16	15	259	16	15	289	16	15	320	16	15	350
17	16	260	17	16	290	17	16	321	17	16	351
18	17	261	18	17	291	18	17	322	18	17	352
19	18	262	19	18	292	19	18	323	19	18	353
20	19	263	20	19	293	20	19	324	20	19	354
21	20	264	21	20	294	21	20	325	21	20	355
22	21	265	22	21	295	22	21	326	22	21	356
23	22	266	23	22	296	23	22	327	23	22	357
24	23	267	24	23	297	24	23	328	24	23	358
25	24	268	25	24	298	25	24	329	25	24	359
26	25	269	26	25	299	26	25	330	26	25	360
27	26	270	27	26	300	27	26	331	27	26	361
28	27	271	28	27	301	28	27	332	28	27	362
29	28	272	29	28	302	29	28	333	29	28	363
30	29	273	30	29	303	30	29	334	30	29	364
—	30	274	31	30	304	—	30	335	31	30	365
—	—	—	—	31	305	—	—	—	—	31	366

TABLE III

Muharram		Safar		Rabi'i		Rabi'ii		Jamada i		Jamada ii	
Day of the		Day of the		Day of the		Day of the		Day of the		Day of the	
Mth.	Year.	Mth.	Year.	Mth.	Year.	Mth.	Year.	Mth.	Year.	Mth.	Year.
1	1	1	31	1	60	1	90	1	119	1	149
2	2	2	32	2	61	2	91	2	120	2	150
3	3	3	33	3	62	3	92	3	121	3	151
4	4	4	34	4	63	4	93	4	122	4	152
5	5	5	35	5	64	5	94	5	123	5	153
6	6	6	36	6	65	6	95	6	124	6	154
7	7	7	37	7	66	7	96	7	125	7	155
8	8	8	38	8	67	8	97	8	126	8	156
9	9	9	39	9	68	9	98	9	127	9	157
10	10	10	40	10	69	10	99	10	128	10	158
11	11	11	41	11	70	11	100	11	129	11	159
12	12	12	42	12	71	12	101	12	130	12	160
13	13	13	43	13	72	13	102	13	131	13	161
14	14	14	44	14	73	14	103	14	132	14	162
15	15	15	45	15	74	15	104	15	133	15	163
16	16	16	46	16	75	16	105	16	134	16	164
17	17	17	47	17	76	17	106	17	135	17	165
18	18	18	48	18	77	18	107	18	136	18	166
19	19	19	49	19	78	19	108	19	137	19	167
20	20	20	50	20	79	20	109	20	138	20	168
21	21	21	51	21	80	21	110	21	139	21	169
22	22	22	52	22	81	22	111	22	140	22	170
23	23	23	53	23	82	23	112	23	141	23	171
24	24	24	54	24	83	24	113	24	142	24	172
25	25	25	55	25	84	25	114	25	143	25	173
26	26	26	56	26	85	26	115	26	144	26	174
27	27	27	57	27	86	27	116	27	145	27	175
28	28	28	58	28	87	28	117	28	146	28	176
29	29	29	59	29	88	29	118	29	147	29	177
30	30	—	—	30	89	—	—	30	148	—	—

TABLE III

Rajab.		Sha'ban.		Ramadan.		Shawwal.		Zul-Qa'da.		Zul-Hijja.	
Day of the		Day of the		Day of the		Day of the		Day of the		Day of the	
Mth.	Year.	Mth.	Year.	Mth.	Year.	Mth.	Year.	Mth.	Year.	Mth.	Year.
1	178	1	208	1	237	1	267	1	296	1	326
2	179	2	209	2	238	2	268	2	297	2	327
3	180	3	210	3	239	3	269	3	298	3	328
4	181	4	211	4	240	4	270.	4	299	4	329
5	182	5	212	5	241	5	271	5	300	5	330
6	183	6	213	6	242	6	272	6	301	6	331
7	184	7	214	7	243	7	273	7	302	7	332
8	185	8	215	8	244	8	274	8	303	8	333
9	186	9	216	9	245	9	275	9	304	9	334
10	187	10	217	10	246	10	276	10	305	10	335
11	188	11	218	11	247	11	277	11	306	11	336
12	189	12	219	12	248	12	278	12	307	12	337
13	190	13	220	13	249	13	279	13	308	13	338
14	191	14	221	14	250	14	280	14	309	14	339
15	192	15	222	15	251	15	281	15	310	15	340
16	193	16	223	16	252	16	282	16	311	16	341
17	194	17	224	17	253	17	283	17	312	17	342
18	195	18	225	18	254	18	284	18	313	18	343
19	196	19	226	19	255	19	285	19	314	19	344
20	197	20	227	20	256	20	286	20	315	20	345
21	198	21	228	21	257	21	287	21	316	21	346
22	199	22	229	22	258	22	288	22	317	22	347
23	200	23	230	23	259	23	289	23	318	23	348
24	201	24	231	24	260	24	290	24	319	24	349
25	202	25	232	25	261	25	291	25	320	25	350
26	203	26	233	26	262	26	292	26	321	26	351
27	204	27	234	27	263	27	293	27	322	27	352
28	205	28	235	28	264	28	294	28	323	28	353
29	206	29	236	29	265	29	295	29	324	29	354
30	207	—	—	30	266	—	—	30	325	—	—